Scriptings of the Soul
In Questions of Light

SIMHANANDA's Little Book of Self-Inquiry
In 308 Contemplative Beads

Simhananda

Printed and bound in Canada by Transcontinental, March 2009

© *Scriptings of the Soul, In Questions of Light* — Simhananda's *Little Book of Self-Inquiry in 308 Contemplative Beads*

ISBN: 978-0-9809694-4-3

© 2009 Orange Palm Publications
First edition Copyright ©1986
Fully re-edited Copyright ©2009

Registration of copyright: First trimester 2009
National Library of Quebec
National Library of Canada

Mailing address: Orange Palm Publications©
235 Rene Levesque Boulevard, Suite 310,
Montreal, Quebec, H2X 1N8
Telephone: (514) 255-8700 ~ Facsimile: (514) 255-0478
E-mail: info@palmpublications.com
Website: http://www.palmpublications.com

Cover photo: Simhananda
Cover design: Lucie Robitaille, Lucie Létourneau
Illustrations: Lucie Robitaille, Lucie Létourneau, Denise Charest
Typesetting: Louise Roy

All rights reserved. No part of this book may be reproduced in any form without permission in writing from the author except to quote, or photocopy specific passages for the purposes of group study.

Publications by Orange Palm Publications:

Our Ordinary Extraordinary Earth and Its Extraordinary Ordinary People. Simhananda. 2008.

Touch To This Earth Where Meanders Mankind. Simhananda. 2008.

Buddhas, Bodhisattvas, Khadromas and the Way of the Pilgrim — A Transformative Book of Photography and Pithy Sayings. Simhananda. 2007.

Holy-Moly Hiccoughs and Enigmatic Knotty Eructations From the Boffola Belly of Bu'Tai— The Drôleries and Dictums of Crazy Modern Dzog-zen. Ken N.O. Sho. 2007.

Knots of Eternity — Paradoxes from Dadi to Daughter. Volume 1. Dadi Darshan Dharma. 2007.

The Smiling Forehead — Paradoxes from Dadi to Daughter. Volume 2. Dadi Darshan Dharma. 2007.

The Great Golden Garland of Gampopa's Sublime Considerations on the Supreme Path — Contemplative Contemporary Commentaries of Gampopa's Root Text. Volume 1. B. Simhananda. 2005.

Forthcoming books:

Paradisal Plums: Peaceful Ponderings from a (Rebel) Pandit's Puce Palm — Aphorisms, Adages, and Analects of Sri Adi Dadi. Volumes 1, 2. Etbonan Karta. Re-edited, updated and expanded version in 2009.

Flyers from the Boys in the Buddhafield. B. Simhananda.

The Great Golden Garland of Gampopa's Sublime Considerations on the Supreme Path. B. Simhananda. Volume 2.

Publications by Magnificent Magus Publications:

The Science of Full Moon Invocations — from Humanity's Heart to Hierarchy's Will; The Divine Concordance of Light III. Dadi Darshan Dharma. 2007.

Seven Studies of Soul Stations or Soul-ar Progressions Upon Each of the Seven Cosmic-Physical Rays; (an integral excerpt from Collectanea One, *The Divine Concordance of Light*). Etbonan Karta. 2007.

Seven Sacred Stations of the Self & Seven Flaming Fiats of Light Upon the Seven Cosmic-Physical Rays (an integral excerpt from *The Divine Concordance of Light*). Etbonan Karta. 2001.

The Divine Concordance of Light: A Handbook from Heaven to Progression Earth —"The Seven Rays of God: Seven Studies of the Soul's Earthly Pilgrimage of Service Upon the Seven Cosmic-Physical Rays". Etbonan Karta. 2001.

Forthcoming books:

The Divine Concordance of Light II: The Science of Invocation and the Art of Affirmation from Station HUMANITY to HIERARCHY'S Heart. Etbonan Karta.

Dedication

To the World's Aspiring
"Little Ones"
and Their Children of Light

Acknowledgement

Eternal gratitude to Shamballa for gracing this enquiring heart with the Wisdom of Its Illimitable Light.

Table of Contents

Foreword xiii

Preface xv

Twenty-Eight Sets of Eleven Contemplative Beads of Divine Inquiry, bringing into play the recurrent use of the word 'LIGHT'.

Chapter I 1
The First Set: THE DIVINE MAN

Chapter II 15
The Second Set: HEAVENWARD JOGGERS

Chapter III 29
The Third Set: WHERE THE WILL OF GOD GOES

Chapter IV 43
The Fourth Set: TWIN ALCHEMICAL MOONS

Chapter V 57
The Fifth Set: OLYMPIAN CARRIER

Chapter VI 71
The Sixth Set: GARMENT OF HOPE

Chapter VII 85
The Seventh Set: ABSOLUTE ZERO-HOOD

Chapter VIII 99
The Eighth Set: IMMERSION AND IMMOLATION

| Chapter IX | . . . . .113 |
| The Ninth Set: | THE EAGLE'S PEAK |

Chapter X 127
The Tenth Set: THE SACRAMENT OF LOVE

Chapter XI 141
The Eleventh Set: DOUBLE-DRUMMED HEARTBEAT

Chapter XII 155
The Twelfth Set: YOUR GOD FRAGRANCE

Chapter XIII 169
The Thirteenth Set: VIOLET SPACES OF SOUL-SOLITUDE

Chapter XIV 183
The Fourteenth Set: AN ONION FIELD OF BUDDHA BRIGHT

Chapter XV 197
The Fifteenth Set: HONG-SAU BREAST

Chapter XVI 211
The Sixteenth Set: HUMBLY AND TALL

Chapter XVII 225
The Seventeenth Set: FOREVER-FRESH AWAKENINGS

Chapter XVIII 239
The Eighteenth Set: YES AND YES AGAIN

Chapter XIX 253
The Nineteenth Set: FALLING AWAKE

Chapter XX 267
The Twentieth Set: LIGHT OF FORGIVENESS

Chapter XXI 281
The Twenty-first Set: FORM, FUNCTION AND FERVOR

Chapter XXII 295
The Twenty-second Set: JUST AS EVERYTHING IS

Chapter XXIII 309
The Twenty-third Set: SPROCKETS OF ETERNITY

The Chapter XXIV 323
The Twenty-fourth Set: ROBE OF HEAVEN

Chapter XXV 337
The Twenty-fifth Set: CHRISTED-BÂTONSHIP

Chapter XXVI 351
The Twenty-sixth Set: INTERDIMENSIONAL LOVING

Chapter XXVII 365
The Twenty-seventh Set: ETERNAL TIME, SYNTHETIC TIME

Chapter XXVIII 379
The Twenty-eighth Set: GOD'S SURPRISED BOSOM

Glossary 393

'So Be the Light in Our Life' Invocation 396

Foreword

Affirmation of life is affirmation of Light.

The human spirit is immortal, but such a simple truth is not close to people; for they care more about the body than about the spirit.

Life obliges man to ascend, whereas death is a descent.

People, in principle, prefer to understand death as destruction. Existence itself affirms eternal renewal. Each man dies for yesterday and is regenerated for tomorrow.

Each day a renewal of all three principles takes place. Each day and hour man draws nearer to or recedes from the Higher World.

Let each one by the quality of his thinking further his own ascent and his perception of the Higher World.

Tranquillity is the crown of the spirit.

People cannot imagine Light as energy.

Let us not look into that Infinity where thought and Light and all that exists merge into unity, but according to the earthly understanding let us apprehend Light as a salutary energy, without which life is impossible.

Light is the most pervasive messenger of salvation.

One can distinctly comprehend a difference between utilitarian fire and cosmic Light. Not fire, but radiance surrounds each living being.

The benevolent thinker is surrounded by a rainbow, and through his light brings healing. So many times We have foretold the future of these radiations. We have said that with such a criterion the very structure of life will be transformed.

One may rightly call Light the principle which leads to regeneration. Thought and Light are so closely linked that thought may be called luminiferous.

Absolutely everything which refers to the luminous future is connected with Light.

Helena Roerich
Excerpt from the book *AUM*

Preface

"Scriptings of the Soul in Questions of Light" is for the seeker and the disciple alike.

"Scriptings" is both a contemplative mode of self-inquiry and a mantra-like medium of thought for the meditative mind.

Would that the Light of the Soul indirectly invoked within these brief indagative queries *awaken* in the reader the dispassion, discrimination and dhyanic discipline needed for a life of conscious work and enlightened service to the all of humanity.

May "Scriptings" help the beauty of your Spirit to literally shine forth from your face in the clear radiance of the Lord's evocative Reply.

Simhananda
February 2, 2009
Montreal, Quebec

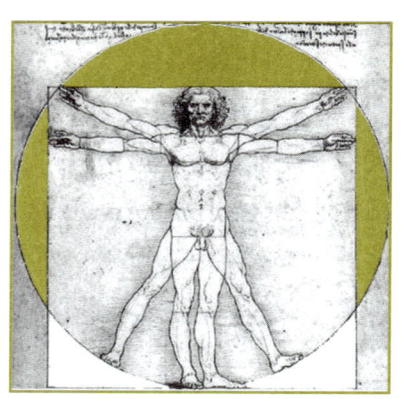

Chapter I

The Divine Man

The First Set
of Eleven Contemplative Beads
of Divine Inquiry, bringing into play
the recurrent use of the word
Light

Questions 1 to 11

Q 1

Light-Flung

Is not the very Soul of man Light-flung from the centre of the All of Life, which is called GOD?

Q 2

Light Fusion

Is not the brilliant core of every man's Being a liberal radiance of refined Light fusion?

Q 3

Light, Love and Life

Is not the essential nature of enlightened Man a subtle commingling of Light, Love and Life?

Q 4

Light and More Light

Does not the Divine Man humbly declare that he is Nothing but an awakened unity of Light and more Light and more Light?

Q 5

Thought, Emotion and Deed

Is not the Divine Man's every thought, emotion and deed consciously imbued with visionary Light and insightful Wisdom?

Q 6

Light-Dipped

Is not the Divine Man's every intent, purpose and proposal, skillfully Light-dipped?

Q 7

Divine Manifestation

Does not even a moment in the company of such a Man full of Light, carry with it the critical Impact and Blessings of a Godly Being in Divine Manifestation?

Q 8

Sands of Time

Are not the words of the Divine Man like piercings of Light scripting through the sands of time?

Q 9

Divine Petals of Grace

Does not such a Man full of Light call down upon Humankind an instant flurrying and quickening of the Divine Petals of Grace?

Q 10

Every Light Footstep

Does not every Light footstep of the Divine Man leave in its wake the tremor of a thousand stars?

Q 11

Will and Desire

Do you man have the will to become such a God of Light?

Do you woman have the desire to become such a Goddess of Light?

Chapter II

Heavenward Joggers

The Second Set
of Eleven Contemplative Beads
of Divine Inquiry, bringing into play
the recurrent use of the word
Light

Questions 12 to 22

Q 12

Path of Return

Is the Incandescent Immensity casting Its clear Light upon your chosen path of Return?

Q 13

Trumpet of Light

Will your battlecry of Rebirth sound forth this time the hallowed trumpet of Light dispelling the darkness?

Q 14

Divine Consciousness

Is your mirror of Light clearly reflecting forth in this very moment, the Divine Consciousness living out the body?

Q 15

Bounty of Light

Does your Bounty of Light brighten up the birds, the bees and even babies?

Q 16

Enlightened Gaze

Does your enlightened gaze transpierce the core of a human being and activate the Divine motor of his own Inner Light?

Q 17

Heavenward Joggers

Does your daily Light-roadwork upon the Spiritual Path brightly inspire fellow Heavenward joggers?

Q 18

Lighted Breath

Is not your Brahman's Breath to become one day
through compassion your brother's Lighted breath?

Q 19

Mantra of Light

Is your creative Mantra of Light not actively helping the world to get rid of the age-old mementos and moldy memory molds often found in the miry marsh of the mean mind, occulted within a crystallized man's lower consciousness?

Renascent Birth

Has your Light Mantra not sweet-swept you as yet, into that wonderful state of Soul expansion, where the ever-fresh and ever-new give renascent birth, to the Ever-Recurring?

Q 21

Sublime Succor

Is the Special Bright of your Inner Light rightly percussing through to your outer life; and is that effulgence of Bright beaming forth a smile of sublime succor upon all sentient beings of temporal Existence?

Q 22

Wound of Separation

Will your integrated Light Self succeed this time around in binding forever the slashing wound of *separation*, thumping omnipresently in people's hearts?

Chapter III

Where the Will of God Goes

The Third Set
of Eleven Contemplative Beads
of Divine Inquiry, bringing into play
the recurrent use of the word
Light

Questions 23 to 33

Will of God

Does not your Light follow resolutely where the Will of God goes?

Q 24

The Great Sun Self

Has your Inner Light Source, the great Sun Self, cleansed you crystal clear of all impure inputs, past and present, through all incarnated levels of the vesselized self?

Q 25

Divine Providence

Has the orbit of your Light become bright and powerful enough to attract the grace and guidance of Divine Providence?

Q 26

Nuts, Bolts and Blocks

Have you attracted and accumulated enough Divine Light in your life to enable you to co-manifest and co-create, in a more conscious cooperation with Spirit, the nuts, bolts and blocks of enlightened daily living?

Q 27

Calling You Home

Have you learnt to really *listen* to the haunting 'O.M.' tones of the Divine Light calling you Home?

Q 28

Mortality and Immortality

Have your daily invocations of Light made you acutely aware of your Mortality, and more importantly still, have they made you truly *remember* your Immortality?

Q 29

Clinging and Cloying

Have your daily Invocations of Light stripped and released you as yet from the clinging and cloying of desire and attachment?

Q 30

Dread of Death

Have your diurnal Invocations of Light really helped to clear from your head the baneful dread of death?

Q 31

The Great Abyss

Has the swooping swoosh and delectable descent of Light from the Godhead permanently filled the great, gainsaying abyss of your inner cravings?

Q 32

Profound View

Is your Light Mirror dust-speckled-free, and does it reflect purely the profound view of God?

Q 33

Divine Alter of Light

Has your consciousness become a Divine Altar of Light upon which the Hierarchy of Masters, the Avatars, the Angels and God can assert the Lila-dance of Life; and through your presently-cleared viable Vessel, can you, this very hour, teach others the Lighted Way?

Chapter IV

Twin Alchemical Moons

The Fourth Set
of Eleven Contemplative Beads
of Divine Inquiry, bringing into play
the recurrent use of the word
Light

Questions 34 to 44

Desire for Godhood

Does your Light rapidly respond at all times, superbly attuned and triumphantly aligned to your perfect desire for Godhood?

Q 35

Himalayan Peaks of Soul

Does the impartial clear-eyed Light of your daily meditations swirl high and bright, beyond the mystical summits of the self to the Himalayan peaks of the Soul?

Q 36

A Humble Tranquility

Does the cool fresh Light of your private meditation, dive down deep and fill the broad valleys of your bosom with a humble Tranquility?

Q 37

Twin Alchemical Moons

Are you sometimes startled when in deep meditation, with the sudden advent of the Light of Knowledge; or, with the vigorous burgeoning of the Buddhic Intuition; or even, with the radiant revelation of the Light of Wisdom?

And beatifically benumbed, do you just sit, anzen-like, and gaze limpidly into the twin alchemical moons of Bliss and Ecstasy?

Q 38

Every Move and Gesture

Is your every move and gesture imbued with the mystique of the Light, and the mystery of more Light?

Q 39

Tranquil Divinity

Does the Light's tranquil Divinity flow radiant and strong from your face?

Q 40

Gentle Power

Does the Light's gentle power flow dynamically but softly from your footsteps?

Q 41

Love for God

Does the Light emanating brightly from your eyes, shine with but Love for God, serving man?

Q 42

Every Sentient Being

Does not the Light-within-the-Light make your body-being glow with Love for every sentient being and living creature, for every pulsating particle and vibrating form?

Q 43

Always

Are you always in the Light and with the Light, as the Light is always with you, and in you?

Q 44

In Short

In short, have you Become as yet the Light?

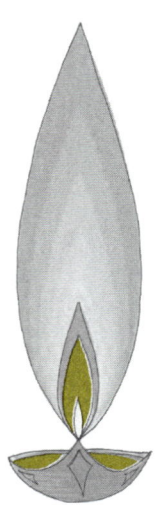

Chapter V

Olympian Carrier

The Fifth Set
of Eleven Contemplative Beads
of Divine Inquiry, bringing into play
the recurrent use of the word
Light

Questions 45 to 55

Q 45

A Spot-Lighted Incarnation

Are you able to stand the test of a spot-Lighted incarnation?

Q 46

Inner Sun

Is not everyone destined to see the birth of their Inner Sun at the exact moment when the small-self merges itself *sacrificially* with the Light of the Exalted Self?

Q 47

This Lifetime Around

Are you determined and dauntless enough this lifetime around to see the full Light of your Self tracing footsteps of cheer and joy into the very dust of the earth?

Q 48

Point-Vanishing

Will you ever see the flash of the small self in flight, point-vanishing egoless into the Light?

God's Divine Play

Will you in this lifetime ever be able to see the Sun Self of your Greater Light dancing out God's Divine Play unto the stage of your ordinary day?

Q 50

Precious Prism

Are you with steadfastness and discipline able to focus the Light of Heaven through the oh-so precious *prism* called your ordinary life?

Q 51

Perch of Perception

Does the profound view of SELF Light naturally permute your present perch of perception in life, regardless of preoccupation, provision, fate, or happening?

Q 52

God's Holy Name

Do you consciously make the effort to invoke forth your Divine Light nature?

Do you always endeavor to remember the adventure of God's Holy Name, hidden behind every name?

Q 53

Watchful Consciousness

Do you consciously, every day, invite and awaken the God Light within your Heart, so that it permeates every pore of your watchful consciousness?

Q 54

Sprinkled Salt

Is your Light serving to lift diamond-sparkling unto the Heavens, the sprinkled salt of the earth consciousness?

Olympian Carrier

Will you not be an Olympian Carrier of the Sacred Flame of Light to all corners of everywhere at all times?

Chapter VI

Garment of Hope

The Sixth Set
of Eleven Contemplative Beads
of Divine Inquiry, bringing into play
the recurrent use of the word
Light

Questions 56 to 66

Q 56

Garment of Hope

Can you sow the discipline of the Discipleship of Light into the hem of Humanity's garment of Hope?

Q 57

Might Tender-Like

Will the Light reflecting compassionately off the wings of your Spirit succeed to make Might tender-like?

Q 58

Angelic Wings

Does the Light of your Soul's angelic wings take flight from the blight of tainted fellowship?

Q 59

Love-Light Droplets

Can your Bird of Light steal to the supernal skies of the Soul and prevail upon It to rain down from the Sun-laughter of the Glad Gods, barrels of Love-Light droplets upon the bent shoulders and grave demeanor of Humanity?

Q 60

Hie Away Forever

Can the God/Goddess Bird of Light within, skyburst, freepike and hie away forever from the grave morass of low-flying minds and the ubiquitous gray clouds, of crass mass-molds?

Q 61

Soul's Bird of Light

Can your Soul's Bird of Light break away from the ponderous human gray and fly high, naturally Divine and Form-Free?

Q 62

Infinitude of Perfection

Will your body-Temple borrowed from the Template of the Living God reach its infinitude of Perfection, through the applied science of a consciously directed stream of Light-thought, playing constantly, coherently, and cogently upon the etheric matrix of matter?

Q 63

Bless and Be

Does the Light in your Heart just Bless and Be and not criticize, admonish, or condemn?

Q 64

Gift of Time

Will the spontaneous Light of your momentary Being propagate the precious gift of Time, wisely-wafted and properly-disbursed in Space?

Q 65

Dispel the Dross

Can your newly-found Light of Grace effortlessly dispel the ponderous dross of the ages caught?

Q 66

Persistent Pulse

Can the persistent pulse of the Divine Light within your Heart, prevail upon all craving and grasping, dependence and addiction?

Chapter VII

Absolute Zero-Hood

The Seventh Set
of Eleven Contemplative Beads
of Divine Inquiry, bringing into play
the recurrent use of the word
Light

Questions 67 to 77

The Long Ago

Has your Light buried the long ago and let go of yesterday's brittle bones?

Q 68

Seriousness of Life

Has your Light yet cracked the seriousness of life with a smile of constant Delight?

Q 69

The Kid-in-You

Has the Light of God, despite its sinuous interpretation and convoluted expression in the wrinkle-browed adult world, yet made the kid-in-you brightly reappear?

Q 70

Matter and Gravity

Is your Light, light-heartedly lightening the gross mental weight of matter; and is your Light, positively alleviating the natural gravity of the worldly life?

Q 71

Meditative Treasure

Has the Crystal Lodestar which is the pure God-Light within you, become a meditative treasure of sweet Blessings for you, in your dual quest as an earnest seeker of Truth and a persistent pursuer of Peace?

Q 72

Assuage the Anguish

Does the Beacon of Light that you are splay through the dark of night and seek to assuage the anguish, the suffering and karmic shipwreckings of fine mortal Souls?

Q 73

The Truth-Thirsty

Do sighs of salvation and of being saved from the limiting hold of matter, Light-catch in the parched throats of the Truth-thirsty, as they near the Presence in you?

Q 74

A Haven and Cathedral

Has the Templed-Light of your Consciousness become a sweet haven of Higher Learning for the intellectual many; and for the selective few, a veritable cathedral of Golden Wisdom?

Q 75

A Healing Source

Has your *transparency* as a broad Being of Light become a healing source of constant comfort and spiritual regeneration for all who humbly come to rest upon its Lordly breast?

Q 76

Heavenly Declarations

Does your Light motherly meet the five elements and melt, merge and metamorphose them into manifest demonstrations of Heavenly Declarations?

Absolute Zero-hood

Can an Arrow of Light zing from the bow of your Buddhahood and bing with creative tension through the bull's eye of the Divine Circle, (without-a-perimeter), straight into the solid emptiness of Absolute Zero-hood?

Chapter VIII

Immersion and Immolation

The Eighth Set
of Eleven Contemplative Beads
of Divine Inquiry, bringing into play
the recurrent use of the word
Light

Questions 78 to 88

Q 78

Mind's Fiery Awakening

Doe the Great Pyramid of your Master Light bid you enter now without further postponement, into the occult Initiatory Chambers of the Mind's Fiery Awakening?

Q 79

Immersion and Immolation

Does the God-Light radiating within you, claim your total Immersion and Immolation into that Love-Flame, which transmutes wholly the 'all that you are' into the 'All That Is'?

Q 80

Perpetual Impulse

Should not the powerful Point of Light which is your present Existence eventually enkindle the living flame of personal Creation into a perpetual impulse of Self-Inspiration?

Q 81

Sweet Strains

Are your unceasing prayers communing with no other Music than the sweet strains of Light?

Q 82

River of Light

Are you positively sure that you are actually casting with open palm and absolute abandon, all of Life's many trials and troubles into the healing waters of God's River of Light?

Q 83

Obviously and Everywhere

Has the Wisdom of your Light not yet broken through the tight lie of those ideas and ideals which section off the Self from 'That Which Is', obviously and everywhere GOD?

Q 84

Perfect Timing

Do you always listen to the Wisdom-Light within, with the total trust that the right resolution, the correct answer and the proper direction will alight confidently and creatively to the surface, with the perfect timing that can only be of God's Knowing?

Q 85

Solidly Existent

Has the Wisdom-Power of your Light shining upon the Path brought to you the Divine reconciliation of the small-self, (with its endless unsubstantial activities), to an alternatively natural state of radically superior BEINGNESS... consisting of effortless effort, non-doing and non-action... and exhibiting the transcendental tranquility of a primary Pristineness, which surprisingly, is found to be essentially empty, but solidly Existent?

Q 86

Disciplinary Disciple-Light

Have you, the sadhaka, meditatively asked your Teacher, Guru or Master, for the desirable descent of the disciplinary Disciple-Light... of wholehearted effort, impeccable order and occult obedience, vis-à-vis your dharma practice and spiritual aspiration of arriving at a true state of Self Liberation upon the noble Initiatory Path?

Q 87

Disciple of Life

Have you commanded the Sweet Lord to solidly implant within you the Light seeds of gentle Strength, compassionate Wisdom and illumined Love, which are the living signs of the true Disciple of Life?

Q 88

"It's All One"

Has the Golden Yarn of Light winding its playful way through the aggregate of personal and impersonal experiences, positive and negative polarities, subjective and objective realities, and all of which may be about 'a-this' or 'a-that', not yet yielded its secret coffers of "It's All One" to you?

Chapter IX

The Eagle's Peak

The Ninth Set
of Eleven Contemplative Beads
of Divine Inquiry, bringing into play
the recurrent use of the word
Light

Questions 89 to 99

… Q 89

Sight and Insight

Does not God as Light give us Sight, and therefore, rouse us to embody a path of Heart and inject a more passionate perspective into life?

Does not God as Light give us Insight, and thereby, prompt us to portray a more profound experience of life, and conjointly, display a greater percipience of Reality, concerning Life?

Q 90

God-Conjoined

Is not the Light within me God-conjoined to the Light within you?

Q 91

A Serious Contact

Does not a serious contact with the Light within, bid you awaken from the robot sleep of the small-self and attend reflectively, actively and simultaneously, to both the potential and transcendental reality of Consciousness?

Q 92

Passing Moment

Does not Light especially serve to empower the mere passing moment with the Buddhic Radiance of CONSCIOUSNESS?

Q 93

Divine Nectar

Is not God as Light forever blessing and filling the individual consciousness with His Divine Nectar?

Q 94

Self-Moved

Is not the Light of Consciousness causally SELF-moved?

Dream of Form

Is not the Light of Self innately Ignorant of the dream of form; and therefore, Is, and remains, (always and originally), fundamentally Free?

Q 96

Divine Innocence

Does not the light-blue Light of God colour the sky of consciousness with the bright bare blush of Divine Innocence?

Natural Joy

Does not a Heart of Happiness give rise
to more and more Fiery Light, radiating forth
in unconstrained promptings of Natural Joy?

Q 98

The Eagle's Peak

Does not the Sacred Circuit of Light travelling in awakened constancy between the Head and Heart, carry into one's life the quintessential contact with That LOVE which begat all worlds and permeates them still, Lovingly-on-Fire from the Eagle's Peak of High Indifference?

Q 99

Real Contact

Should not a real contact with the Light lay to rest all quests, including that of Spiritual seeking?

Chapter X

The Sacrament of Love

The Tenth Set
of Eleven Contemplative Beads
of Divine Inquiry, bringing into play
the recurrent use of the word
Light

Questions 100 to 110

… Q 100

Master Bouquet

Has your Soul Light yet released a Master Bouquet of Life's aromatic truths to you?

Q 101

Clear Knowing

Has your Soul Light whispered to you the clear Knowing that you are not that which you emote, think and do; and neither, of course, are you that which lives and dies?

Q 102

Sole Self

Has your Soul Light made you acutely aware that you are the sole SELF which *oversees* all dichotomous viewpoints?

Q 103

Silent Solar Witness

Has your Soul Light yet demonstrated to you that you are in truth the High-Seeing SELF, that *Silent Solar Witness*, who washes away to sheer limpidity all struggling dualities, in the winnowing turf of God's Unitive Grace?

Q 104

The Tisra Til

Have your daily invocations to the Light of SELF tender-touched, tapped and toned the Tisra Til, the Third Eye?

Q 105

Earth's Little Children

Has the steadfast invocation of the Light of S<small>ELF</small> in daily meditation brought to you as yet that advanced degree of disciplined discipleship, where the giving of your single-minded attention to the Spirit of G<small>OD</small> flows as Divine Love, and rains down as a gentle Compassion falling timelessly upon all of Earth's little children?

Q 106

Desire-Abyss

Has the swooping swoosh of Silence and the dove-like descent of continuous Light from the Godhead, clearly, collectedly and calmly filled the great Desire-Abyss of your inner cravings and outer passions?

Q 107

Cries of Delusion

In the steadfast lifting of your eyes toward the Light of the SOUL, have the dark chimeras of your Being yet cawed out their last forlorn cries of delusion?

Q 108

Occult Crux

Can you openly, confidently and vulnerably hold to your bosom of Light the God-trusting moment-of-Now, tenderly-tucked into the occult crux of your consecrated hollow hand?

Q 109

The Weighty Clam

Will the Light of your Being eventually proffer to you the great occult pearl of Buddhic Intuition, bereft of the weighty clam of knowledge?

Q 110

Sacrament of Love

Can you in deep meditation raise the sacredness of the Moment high above your head like the Holy Host of a Guru-Full-Moon... beaming down Light beams of Compassion into a world dying for the Sacrament of Love?

Chapter XI

Double-Drummed Heartbeat

The Eleventh Set
of Eleven Contemplative Beads
of Divine Inquiry, bringing into play
the recurrent use of the word
Light

Questions 111 to 121

Q 111

And Yet...

Does not the daily practice of Light meditation declaim that nothing is of importance, and yet, the all of it is Extraordinary?

Q 112

Planetary Star

Has the Light succeeded in establishing within you your own private far-away planetary star, where the all of life is safe and O.K., and you feel God-secured and far-removed from the incessant pull-and-push of the world?

Q 113

Creation of a Pomegranate

Even in the midst of loud noise and rampant activity, are you wisely allowing yourself the practice of turning your gaze ever-inwards, toward your precious planet of subjective Light... where only you and God commune in Love and share together the secret creation of a pomegranate?

Q 114

Double-Drummed Heartbeat

Does the Soundless Light within your breast recognize Itself as an intense tiny Flame, burning eternally golden-bright within the right Bliss Conduit of your Double-Drummed Heartbeat?

Q 115

Deep Peace

Does your Heart full of Light and your Spirit full of Joy make other hearts pause and skip a beat, and wonder why they are left with a peculiar feeling of unaccounted Deep Peace?

Q 116

Change

Does the Light within your Heart help you to embrace change so totally, that change itself is Changed?

Q 117

Full to the Brim

Does the Blissful Light of the Heart not want to make you die this very moment upon a single sigh of 'O.M.', full to the brim of Divine Whatevers?

Q 118

Shattered Shards

Has the One S͟ELF's pristine flash of Monadic Light, spontaneously slashed the Sun of your Consciousness into shattered shards of God Illumination?

Q 119

God's Great Garage

Do you periodically go out in Consciousness to God's Great Garage in the Sky and ask for a cosmic Light Change, Love Check and Will-Alignment, vis-à-vis the physical form and other (subtle) bodies of your Being?

Q 120

Monkey Busy-ness

Do you feel that your growing Circle of Light is making real headway toward the gradual Mastery of the meandering mind's monkey busy-ness?

Q 121

Thought-Prattle

Is the Soul's Light categorically achieving through ever-expanding circles of Inner Quiet, in cutting-down on the mind's ceaseless prattle, regardless of whether the particular thought-prattle be something just plain, or something plainly profound?

Chapter XII

Your God Fragrance

The Twelfth Set
of Eleven Contemplative Beads
of Divine Inquiry, bringing into play
the recurrent use of the word
Light

Questions 122 to 132

Q 122

The Purling Sound

Does your pearl of Light prod awake the purling Sound of God in the human breast of each extemporaneous encounter you make?

Q 123

Lovely Billows

Does your Light ignite the hoary embers of Sacred Horizons in those aspiring Souls who are eagerly awaiting to burst Divinely-ablaze upon the lovely billows of your God Fragrance?

Q 124

In True Humility

As a full-fledged Spiritual Warrior and Lover of the Light, are you in true humility rendering to others the valuable service and golden opportunity of your legitimate and compassionate Light Presence?

Q 125

The Sacred Enigma

Have you not yet unmasked the Sacred Enigma that the whole webbing of Life is related to your Light?

Q 126

Experiential Space

Is not your Soul Light spiritually spiraling multi-dimensionally on and on, in an exciting ever-expanding, exponential exploration of Experiential Space?

Q 127

Immutable Void

Is not your Soul Light ever dreaming to one fine day be able to span the bridge of time and break-out in full Beingness, into the Immortality of the Immutable Void?

Q 128

Original Abode

Is it not true that the Soul and Its Light earnestly desire to lure man back upwards to his Real roots, into the bluest Infinitude of his Original Abode?

Q 129

Mellowed Gold

Has your Innate Light not yet finely melded together and fused into mellowed gold the psyche and the Soul, the personality and the Spirit, the human being and God?

Q 130

Road-Runner Beeps
And Hurricane Lanes

Has your Lake of Light-Calm and its companion Pond of Peace not yet freed your Consciousness from the raucous road-runner beeps and hurricane lanes of human hustle and horde arousal?

Q 131

Divine Amrita

Has your Buddha Light yet become likened to a perfumed field of heavenly wildflowers, qualifying the air of thought and Consciousness, with the Divine Amrita of purity, goodness and innocence?

Q 132

Angelic Ignorance

Does not the Heavenly Light sing to your Soul solely in the higher octaves of Angelic Ignorance?

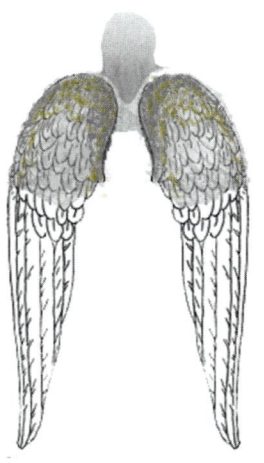

Chapter XIII

Violet Spaces of Soul-Solitude

The THIRTEENTH SET
of Eleven Contemplative Beads
of Divine Inquiry, bringing into play
the recurrent use of the word
LIGHT

Questions 133 to 143

Q 133

Converging of the Light

Has the converging of the Light upon you ushered in as yet, the inevitable and irrevocable conviction of: "What else Truly matters"?

Q 134

'On-the-Scene' Samsara

Have you noticed that the Light of the Genuine Self sweeps simultaneously out at once from the four cardinal corners of Creation, to purposefully and compassionately connect the elusive moment to the Reality of Being... thereby, 'Lighting-up' life at once with the momentous miracle and prompt empowerment of the personal *now*, within a current cycle of some illusive 'on-the-scene' *samsara*?

Q 135

Cosmic Womb

Is not faltering Humanity's spiritual training in learning how to abide steadfastly and sure within the tranquil Centre of the Light throughout all of the diverse highs and lows of life, not a positive harbinger that a whole new age of Godly Beings are forthwith being seeded, in the Cosmic Womb of the Aquarian Mother of Light?

Q 136

Symphony of Creation

Are not the seven ascending and descending Cosmic-Physical Rays of the CREATOR's rainbowed octave of Light, the perfect visual and harmonic accompaniment, to His Primal-Sounding of the Symphony of Creation?

Q 137

Reed of God

From out of the holes and hollowness of the lonely Reed of God, does not your ensouled Divinity Light-burst forth into manifestation, upon the Pure Sound of the universal note of LOVE?

Q 138

God's Golden Eagle

Do not the two Great Wings of GOD's Golden Eagle, the Light and the Sound, (or the Bright and the Shabd), beat-out hushly and still into the subtle Inner Sky a shrill *Omkar* call... therewith, invoking the Soul's ready return to Heaven's Home via the blazing blue Lane of Love, or the candent Red Corridor of Compassion?

Q 139

Light Summon

Is not Maitreya the Christ as Holy Hierarchy's officially-appointed World Instructor, resplendently sounding a Light Summon to all, to come take the Darshan Blessing of his Universally-incarnated, Light Form?

Q 140

Invisible Wind

From out of the All Alone is it not the Lord's Light which swooshes forth as an Invisible Wind, searing *shunyata-like* through the Silence?

Q 141

Dream Vision

Is it not the Supreme Lord's Light which thunder-splintered the Void and cast forth into Form the coloured Dream Vision of our multi-splendoured world?

Q 142

Soul-Solitude

Does not the Light of S̶ᴇʟꜰ occultly shine-on, from out of the long violet spaces of Soul-solitude?

Q 143

Listening to the Light

Does not the "peace which passeth all understanding", come about by longingly sitting through many a distant, satin nights of God-Stillness, just listening to the Light?

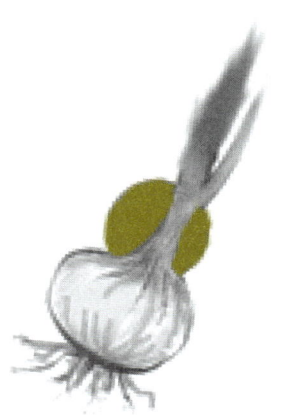

Chapter XIV

An Onion Field of Buddha Bright

The Fourteenth Set
of Eleven Contemplative Beads
of Divine Inquiry, bringing into play
the recurrent use of the word
Light

Questions 144 to 154

Q 144

Remembering

Is not the end of forgetting the Light of Remembering?

Q 145

Non-Being, Non-Doing

Is not the Light of Emptiness, the Fullness of Non-Being.

Is not the Light of Effortlessness, the Bliss of Non-Doing?

Q 146

'Overshadowing Governing Good'

Is not the Light of TRUTH inherently present, singularly recognized, and especially evoked in the Principle of the Unicity of Life which implodes everywhere-binding, the universal energy of Love, and lays down everywhere-espoused for the future, the favorable imposition of the venerable Law of the 'Overshadowing Governing Good'?

Q 147

Ladder of Humility

Is it not a fact that the further a man ascends up the ladder of Humility the greater his Light burns bright, and the greater, (and safer), his potency becomes in his Love for the Christ?

Q 148

The Loving Light

Is it not obvious that the Soul in being constituted primarily of Light and Love, can only be rightly beheld by one whose personality is becoming the Loving Light?

Q 149

The "I-Passions"

Does not hate, anger, jealousy, desire, bondage and delusion obviously obscure the Light-within; yet, why does man go on blindly arousing the "I-passions", which make him suffer so, in egotistical discord with his Soul... all wrapped-up in self-importance, (gluttonous) self-esteem, narcissistic vainglory, disharmony and dis-ease?

Q 150

Conscious Dying

As long as you are endeavoring to live in the Light of greater conscious Living, why not also go for the Light of conscious Dying?

Q 151

Daily Dying

Since death marks the ultimate liberation of our particle consciousness into the eternal Light of Spirit, should we not then, seriously practice the meditative discipline of daily dying into that Light?

Q 152

Face of Death

Often, as death approaches, and this, despite the experiential process of having undergone much intense suffering, the golden-white Light remains all the while with the pulsating pain of the patient, as bright and Brighter and light and Lighter, the Luminescence becomes.

Oddly and mysteriously, the Light seems, (sometimes), to transform the very face of Death itself.

Can it be so?

Q 153

Open Heartspaces

Is it not the Love of the Lord which 'lives and moves and fills the whole of my Being'; and is it not His penetrative Light which sees with Agape, through the open heartspaces of little 'ole me?

Q 154

Buddha Bright

As the darkness of death detonates into Light, why not free-fall into an onion field of Buddha Bright?

Chapter XV

Hong-Sau Breast

The Fifteenth Set
of Eleven Contemplative Beads
of Divine Inquiry, bringing into play
the recurrent use of the word
Light

Questions 155 to 165

Q 155

Anchor and Polarize

Does not the steadfast focussing of our consciousness within the Soul principally serve to anchor and polarize the small self to an ever-increasing amount of Self Light?

Q 156

Divine Fullness

Is not Divine Fullness the realization of the Soul joyfully Loving all within the arrayed Divine Heptachord, or rainbowed Light of God?

Q 157

Impregnate the Sky

Is not the Light of the Soul constantly seeking to impregnate the sky of our Consciousness with the One Thought of GOD?

Q 158

Hong-Sau Breast

Does the conscious shinning of your Light not prod awake the humming Sound-of-God in the Hong-Sau breast of the aspiring man?

Q 159

Questionable Necessity

Do you not believe that the inherent Immortality of your Light will make of your death a merry mockery; to the point of taking note of it as merely being a natural process... of somewhat questionable necessity?

Q 160

Absolute Will

Is not Absolute Will sounding forth the Plan of God, for the specific purpose of progressive mortal transformation into the Light?

Q 161

Light Alchemy

Are not mastery in Meditation and authority in Invocation,
the twin crystal chords of transformative Light alchemy?

Q 162

Living Christos Light

Is not the living Christos Light the unique passage of Way to our extraordinary possibility-in-God?

Q 163

Convoluted Riddles

Does not the cumulative effect of meditative potency being generated within the Light, become at some crucial contemplative point, the sadhaka's spear of cardinal discernment and his primary promontory of profound perspective, in the efficient handling of Life's convoluted riddles?

Q 164

Old Mystical Triangle

Is not the disciplined disciple's consciousness in this Aquarian Age critically amassing Light, the aggregate of which is leading him to a most definite tipping-over, of the old mystical triangle of Pisces?

Q 165

Enlightened Relevancy

Is not the present impulse of Humankind's Heart directed toward an intelligent comprehension of the interrelatedness of both Divine and earthly forces; and does not Mankind desire more and more a peaceful resolution to the conflicting interests of world situations and events; and is this not a flashing indicator of Humanity's readiness in the Light, to let Holy Hierarchy usher in a brand new age of Enlightened Relevancy?

Chapter XVI

Humbly and Tall

The Sixteenth Set
of Eleven Contemplative Beads
of Divine Inquiry, bringing into play
the recurrent use of the word
Light

Questions 166 to 176

Q 166

Every Single Thing

Is not every single thing in life either a simple fact,
or complex chain-artifact, of crystallized Living Light?

Q 167

Re-Creates Anew

Is it not the Light which creates; is it not the Light which preserves; is it not the Light which destroys every form, and then, re-Creates everything anew?

Q 168

Waters of Life

Is not absolutely everything but a cryptic, dynamic descending and nubiferous moving of the Light upon the waters of Life?

Q 169

Boat of Light

My brother and sister, have you not yet learned to row your boat of Light implacably upon the aleatory, unsteady waters of life?

Q 170

Humbly and Tall

Whenever you feel a gentle push or subtle tug of the Light beckoning, do you follow its bidding willingly; and do you readily go wheresoever it goes, doing so Argus-eyed, humbly and tall?

Q 171

Abiding Light

Does not sentient compassion for man arise from the special Heart whose Love blazes forth naturally as abiding Light?

Q 172

Omega Light, Alpha Love

Is not the crowning act of a man's life the climatic consummation of all human frailty and the total transmogrification of his human heart into the terminal finality of his realized Omega Light... in close concord with the immortal *spanda*, or pulsing eternal spring, of the Monad's Alpha LOVE?

Q 173

'Naught But God'

Is it not natural that at one crucial point in your spiritual evolution upon the Path, the Divine Light will give you instead of death, the choice of Living on in the form, (in consciously expanded-time); selflessly serving man and carrying high the flambeau of Divinity, for all those veritable seekers whose special request is 'Naught but God'?

Q 174

Circumvolving Light

Are you ready to die one last time and become vibrantly alive with the holy waters of your sacred stream of circumvolving Light?

Q 175

Monadic Reality

Will you ever intimately know the dreaded, definite drowning of the small self; and consequently, realize the resolute taking-up of the active life of the Soul... all the way directly into the transparent, transcendental Light of Monadic Reality?

Q 176

Being-Here-Now

Can one ever be so totally, so absolutely and so lovingly blessed by the Light... as can only be possible in the exquisitely, blissful state of Being-Here-Now?

Chapter XVII

Forever-Fresh Awakenings

The Seventeenth Set
of Eleven Contemplative Beads
of Divine Inquiry, bringing into play
the recurrent use of the word
Light

Questions 177 to 187

Q 177

Cross of Light

How is it that the Breadth of Existence expands and contracts upon the rhythmic breath of Light, and mystifyingly draws its circumference about a cryptic, equal-armed Cross of Light?

Q 178

Exalted Intent

How is it that the Breath of Life is trumpeted gloriously upon the exalted intent of the Logoic Light?

Q 179

White Spirituality

Is not fusion of the small self with the lofty Light of the Higher Self a practical, necessary, scientific step to be seriously taken by the individual seeker upon the modern, innovative 'Invocative Path' to contemporary White Spirituality?

Q 180

Unremitting Immensity

Is it not an important part of the Soul's spiritual practice to Light-connect by means of occult meditation and practical pranic exercise, the physically-elusive moment of Now to its Spiritual counterpart, which is the infinitely gracing moment of (the) Eternal Now, to be hermetically found in the great unremitting IMMENSITY?

Q 181

Fatherly Solicitation

Is it not the Fatherly solicitation of the MONAD, which propels the Light of the Soul to fuse, unify and merge with the Reality of LIFE?

Q 182

Very Special Place

Is not everyone destined to find that very secret place within the reverberant beingness of the Clear Light; that very special place, which is quintessentially made of forever-fresh awakenings and sheer stupendous, spontaneous revelations?

Q 183

'Conscious Cooperation'

Will there not come a time in the not-so-distant future when the Universal Light of Mankind will explicitly create Creation in 'conscious cooperation' with that Summital Being, who is considered to be 'our Father who art in Heaven'?

Q 184

True Dawning

Is not the light of the earthly dawn but a mere reflective ritual, a daily rebirth, a sun-dance, or symbolic representation in Nature of the true dawning of the Light of Soul, within the systemic process of a man's eventual, evolutionary Awakening?

Q 185

Whose Name Is Multitude

In the primal importance of caring for the plight of any Soul hungering to be nurtured in Spirit, is the Light-within not also reminding each one to perhaps reach out a physical hand, and if capable, feed any found empty belly; and just mayhaps, treat the suffering of the manifest form of those sentient beings whose name is multitude, and are known to live scantily and neglected in the world, as the Lord's destitute creatures?

Q 186

Initiatory Younger

Are we not as moral and conscious members of the Bright Brotherhood, compassionately called to take Lightly upon us under cape and cover of terrestrial night, the suffering and plight of all those souls who are initiatory younger in Light?

Q 187

Light Brotherhood

Can you envision the Christ as the New World Instructor, inspiriting a fresh fusion of all human souls into a scientific Light Brotherhood of shared wealth, practical peace and joyful service to be impartially bestrewed amongst all of God's sentient creatures?

Chapter XVIII

Yes and Yes Again

The Eighteenth Set
of Eleven Contemplative Beads
of Divine Inquiry, bringing into play
the recurrent use of the word
Light

Questions 188 to 198

The Lord's Plan

Should not the Lord's Plan and His Willed Intent,
be one day Light-intuited by the disciplined disciple?

Q 189

'Yes and Yes Again'

Does not the Wisdom of saying 'yes and yes again', to both Light and Life, adduce more and more of the Light, to more and more of Life?

Q 190

Mystical Mists

Does not the flawless Truth which is clear unalloyed Light, cut skillfully and cleanly through the mystical mists of the enslaved and enthralled, kama-manasic mind?

Q 191

Lighted Peak

Will not man inexorably realize, one day soon, the limitless expanse of the Infinite Whole, from the Lighted peak of his own Higher Mind?

Q 192

Obfuscated Lanes

Why not drive your Spirit vehicle consciously, by utilizing the Light of Soul to illumine the obfuscated lanes of Life?

Q 193

Sunportals

Is the bright shinning of your Light softly pulse-waving open the sunportals of your Brother's consciousness?

Q 194

Arc of Light

Does the Disciple's path to Freedom not demand the disciplined building of a rainbowed Arc of Light, from the initiating Alpha-point of the Soul to the realized Omega-luminosity of his *jivatmic* Self?

Q 195

Saintly Man

Does not a Celestial Light surround in beautiful nimbic scintillation the blessed crown of a saintly Man?

Q 196

Perrenial Wisdom

Could it, in fact be, that the Light of Wisdom never really evolves, but it is rather the human being who evolves and unfolds toward the ever-brightening Light; and that, in his fervent quest to become one with that Light, his aggregate of Luminescence fructifies into the perrenial Wisdom which already Is, ever Was and will Be?

Q 197

'Group Meditation'

Is not the time quickly encroaching upon Man when the consolidating and catalysing agency of 'Group Meditation', will become more and more consciously attuned by him and will be sounded the world over, in unison to the Lighted Purpose of DIVINE WILL?

Q 198

Brand New Dawn

Could not the successful rising of a single Son of Man into the Light, also point to the parallel unfoldment of a Son of God disappearing ever-higher-and-brighter, into a brand New Dawn of some Cosmic Relevancy?

Chapter XIX

Falling Awake

The Nineteenth Set
of Eleven Contemplative Beads
of Divine Inquiry, bringing into play
the recurrent use of the word
Light

Questions 199 to 209

Q 199

Just Sit and Listen

Do you sometimes take the time to just sit and Listen to the movement of the susurrous Light surging in your Consciousness?

Q 200

Falling 'Awake'

When are you going to transform the practice of falling asleep at night into the ceremony of falling 'Awake' into the Light?

Q 201

Vast Inner Spaces

Is it not your Soul's Light and that Light alone, which can Illumine the vast Inner spaces of your Being?

Q 202

'Naught But That'

Is it not a function of your Innate Purpose to become Light and more Light and more Light, until you become innerly 'Naught but That', as Divine fact?

Q 203

Beam of Life

Would it not be incomparably wonderful to allow the blessed Beam of Life to strike the sounding board of your broad Being, and rouse you to resonate only to the Light of LOVE and the Sound of FREEDOM?

Q 204

Tiniest Created Particle

Is not the tiniest created particle a primordial point of Light penetrating the dark of space?

Q 205

Personality and Psyche

Should not both your personality and psyche become etherically pervaded and spiritually permuted by the Bright of your Light Presence?

Q 206

Critical Point

Does not the steadfast increase of the inner meditative Light within a man's perspective of consciousness, inevitably reach a critical point of self-Transformation?

Q 207

The Peerless Self

Is it not the disciplined duty of a disciple of the 'Religion of Light' to tetrahedronically transfigurize himself into the brilliance of the Peerless Self as 'pure Energy'; and thereupon, be able to perfectly perceive It, to reconceive It, and to recreate It; and thereafter, consciously and selectively, channel It through the projected hologrammic forms of his Soul's gross and subtle bodies?

Q 208

Science of Love

Does not the Spiritual Law state that as you give and give and give of the Light through the sacrifice of the Self in service to others, so shall you be blessed in your stepping up the Ladder of Light into a greater abundance of Grace, and thereupon, into a greater Understanding of the Christly Science of LOVE?

Q 209

Ocean of Light

Would it not be wonderful to have our thinking process and mental sight constantly bathed in the Light, so that, (in time), they would become the substantial constants of Consciousness... and the very Ocean of Light through which we breathe, move and have our being?

Chapter XX

Light of Forgiveness

The Twentieth Set
of Eleven Contemplative Beads
of Divine Inquiry, bringing into play
the recurrent use of the word
Light

Questions 210 to 220

Q 210

Transformative Path

Is not the compassionate Light of practised daily forgiveness both of self and other, absolutely necessary to enable the disciple to take the next truly significant step upon the strenuous Transformative Path?

Q 211

Light of Forgiveness

Does not the practised Light of Forgiveness help in cleansing the windows of Soul from the selfish grime of ego-contamination?

Q 212

A Precious Aid

Is not the Light of Forgiveness a precious aid in keeping the windshield of a man's Consciousness crystal-clear of offensive (kama-manasic) bugs, for a fuller and greater GOD View?

Q 213

Extra Light

Does not the Light of Forgiveness also serve in keeping the daily dharma, (and karma), of Life extra light?

Q 214

Involutionary Purpose

Does not the Light of Forgiveness in meditation help to dematerialize many of the world's mortal admixtures of willful and wayward human accomplishment... most of which smells of separativeness, stinks of selfishness and is physically, (or psychically), stuck to involutionary purpose?

Q 215

Those Contractive Bonds

Does not the increased Light derived from daily forgiveness, free the small-self from going dour, sour, and unforgiving... primarily through the means of promoting a selfish attitude... and spawning an unhealthy attachment for those contractive bonds which the lesser involvements of life tend to generate?

Q 216

Divine Protection

As a child of God's Brightness and a disciple of the Karmaless Wisdom, is not the disciplined practice of standing detached and steadfast within the Light, your best shield of Divine protection against the ventured attacks, barbs and batteries of those wrong deeds and evil doings, which are bound to be directed your way upon the noble and upward Path to Freedom?

Q 217

To Better Serve

Does not the Grace of Greater Light empower you with a Greater Knowing of what precisely it is you need to learn, in order to better serve your fellowman, fellow creatures, and GOD?

Q 218

Higher Octaves

Does not the High S*ELF* sing out its Light to the Souls of men, only in the higher octaves of Christly Love?

Q 219

Will and Whisper

Is your Eye of Light able to perceive the pure wave-length of the Will of God?

Is your Heart of Light able to suffer the thundering roar of the Whisper of God?

Q 220

Tunnel of Love

As a son or daughter of the Universal Light looking out upon all things with Equanimity and Tranquility, has your mystical vision yet bored through the unequivocal Tunnel of Love which looks out dispassionately, yet equipotently, upon the all of LIFE?

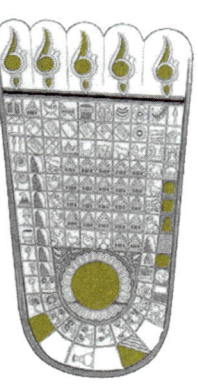

Chapter XXI

Form, Function and Fervor

The Twenty-First Set
of Eleven Contemplative Beads
of Divine Inquiry, bringing into play
the recurrent use of the word
Light

Questions 221 to 231

Q 221

Wonderful

Would it not be wonderful to be able to think all thoughts in their Light-form and to see all things in their mould of Light-energy?

Q 222

Seventh Ray Energy

Would it not be wonderful to see the Soul actively shimmer like a star within mortal flesh, through the Divine Light alchemy of the Seventh Ray energy astutely wielded?

Q 223

A Higher Initiate

Is it not the occult instinct of a Higher Initiate to masterfully control all that a man may be bodily, emotionally, mentally and spiritually... with the subsequent transformation and transfiguration of this total amalgam into the Light... until he in fact, truth, and reality, becomes the Light Radiant?

Q 224

Form, Function and Fervor

Is it not the Divine Fohatic Light which gives Form, Function and Fervor to all of the ten thousand things of Creation?

Q 225

Divine Longings

Is your Consciousness adequately reflecting the Light of the Soul through a fine and clear mind, a pure heart, a strong body and an ample munificence of Divine longings?

Q 226

Raja Yoga

Have you through deep contemplative thought and the spacious practice (of the science) of Raja Yoga, figured out how to sagely utilize the dynamic Light of Meditation to transgress time, and thrust the consciousness of the spirit (boldly) through the vast intra-galactic spaces, to the very heart of that Great Immensity, called GOD?

Q 227

Regenerative Light

Is it not time for the white magic of your regenerative Light to finally and irrevocably, master the hoary illusion of advancing time, and the parallel penumbra of old age?

Q 228

'Relative Zero-Ageing'

Will not the Invocative Light of advanced Spiritual Science produce for mankind a physical body able to be maintained at 'relative zero-ageing' for an indefinite period of Godly Service?

Come-Passionate Music

Is not Compassion the melodious sound of the cosmic impulse of Light, modifying Divine Love into come-passionate music, hallowed for the supra-sensitive ears of the mortal Heart?

Q 230

Softest of Silences

Does not the advent of Light sometimes roll thunderingly-in, and at other times, slip surreptitiously by upon the softest of Silences, to the distant shores of your Contemplative Mind?

Q 231

Alchemical Elixir

Has it perhaps occurred to you that contained within the common 'Light-rainbow' is harbored the quintessential key to physical renewal, psychic regeneration and etheric rejuvenation; and that within the modest bosom of its seven-hued spectrum, there sleeps serenely the esoteric secret of the alchemical elixir to Immortality?

Chapter XXII

Just As Everything Is

The Twenty-Second Set
of Eleven Contemplative Beads
of Divine Inquiry, bringing into play
the recurrent use of the word
Light

Questions 232 to 242

Impersonal Impetus

Is not the Impersonal Impetus to live as Living Light the consummate platform upon which the en-Soul-ed Life can bestir the sacred fires of the personal Being?

Q 233

The Soul

How is it that the Soul serves to brightly enlighten, that is to say, Light-up our personal (egoic) existence, and bind us in the very same breath to the Living Light of eternal time?

Q 234

Maitreya's Presence

As a Warrior of God and Lover of the Light, are you not yet carrying the truth of Maitreya's Presence to others, upon the sacred plate of a detached Consciousness?

Q 235

Ego's Personal Demise

Does not the enlightened Spiritual Man take birth in the Lighted Glory of the 'Sun Self', rising precisely at the dawn of the ego's personal demise?

Q 236

Enamored Reflection

Is not the astral light of a man's desire and devotion but an enamored reflection of his own ideal of Love; and does not his personal bliss concern his own spiritually-biased feeling and emotion, expressed in the specious Light of a nitidously-mirrored Wisdom?

Q 237

Ineffable Light

Why not sincerely, earnestly and non-glamorously seek the Real; why not invoke the non-reflected, Ineffable Light of the immutable Spark of Soul?

Q 238

Everything Is O.K.

Does not Divine Wisdom's knowing 'Eye of Light', bend upon Humanity a powerful and benevolent look of Divine Tranquility, thereby, blessing man and assuring the world and the cosmos that everything is O.K., *just as everything Is?*

Q 239

New World Synthesis

Does not the LORD's Living Look of Light presently encapsulated within the visionary Will of the present Maitreyic Christ, bring Hope for a new world order of Universal Peace; and does He not as the Christ have the cosmic mandate to create a new world synthesis of Spirituality, inspiriting the union of all human souls to join as ONE in a truly religious and scientific Brotherhood, upon the great evolutionary Ladder of Love and the purifying Cross of Light?

Q 240

Disarraying Distress

With the kaleidoscopic canopy of astrally-induced desires and emotions creating inner chaos everywhere, and of astrally-imposed thoughtforms being thrusted pell-mell within a man's mind, is it not, therefore, manifestly normal that Mankind continues to suffer from the disarraying distress of Light instability and Soul sickness?

Q 241

Arrant Glamours

Are not the beautiful bodies and multiple sexual fantasies, chromed charms and acquisitive money mirages of the world, merely arrant glamours which constantly deform and distort the natural Light of the Soul in Its clear vision and pure contemplation of God?

Q 242

Tripartite Enlightenment

Is it not grand to be able to inwardly tune-in and Light-intone in Sound-surround the Hierarchy's 'Great Invocation'... calling for the revolutionary, tripartite enlightenment of Man, in the near-future Golden Age of the Aquarian Dispensation?

Chapter XXIII

Sprockets of Eternity

The Twenty-Third Set
of Eleven Contemplative Beads
of Divine Inquiry, bringing into play
the recurrent use of the word
Light

Questions 243 to 253

Q 243

Absolute Divinity

Is your mushrooming Light beginning to reveal to you the absolute Divinity that you Are?

Q 244

The Manifest

Is the Light of Wisdom not coaxing you ever closer, toward the personal recognition of a shared inter-penetrative, co-creative and co-incarnational coalition with the Manifest, via the awakening realization and appreciation that everyone-everywhere bestows his own particular gift of Beingness, to the ONENESS of it all?

Q 245

High-Intensity Desire

Does not any high-intensity desire for either something, or someone, cause an immediate opaqueness of vision, and an instant blurring of the clear Light of Mind?

Q 246

In Heaven and On Earth

Is it not an immediate part of your plan and purpose in life, to become appreciated both in heaven and on earth as an awakened Child of the Light?

Microcosmic and Macrocosmic

Are not all microcosmic and macrocosmic worlds Light-activated by the universal, binding and pervasive power of the WILL, mindfully affixed to the intelligence of an Enlightened Love?

Q 248

The Human Heart

Does the human heart not aspire to its natural contemplative pulse by meditating with greater depth and pure mindfulness on that modern Master Beacon... who is the Twin Soul and Occult Brother of the Enlightened Buddha, and whose Name is the LORD MAITREYA and whose universal Inspiriting Light is... known ecumenically, as the CHRIST Light?

Q 249

All There Is

Does the steady practice of holding one's sight steadfast in the Light not disclose to one's Soul, the manifest revelation that God-the-Whole is *all there Is?*

Q 250

Sprockets of Eternity

Won't an increased Inner Light patiently unravel the great jigsaw puzzle of time-space, and lay bare for you the very sprockets of Eternity upon the present stage of your Life mystery?

Q 251

Friend

Will the where, when and why of the dark of night
ever greet the clear Light of day, and call it Friend?

Q 252

Nebulous Nothing

Is the Light of Spirit not destined to dispel the dark of matter and send it back scurrying into the shadows of that nebulous Nothing from whence it came?

Q 253

Undiminished Quest

Does not the evolutionary man upon Knowing the SELF, shy instantaneously away from the past eternity of bygone moments of Grace; and does he not proceed purposefully, to ascend from what seemed the summit of his Soul to yet another greater Peak of Light, in his undiminished quest to meet the All Alone?

Chapter XXIV

Robe of Heaven

The Twenty-Fourth Set
of Eleven Contemplative Beads
of Divine Inquiry, bringing into play
the recurrent use of the word
Light

Questions 254 to 264

Q 254

Robe of Heaven

Is not the unconditioned Light the undisclosed fabric of the Robe of Heaven, which God dons for Creation?

Q 255

Phenomenal Corridor

Does your unfurling Light not assist in boring a passageway to God through the phenomenal corridor of time-space?

Q 256

Ample Abundance

Does the Treasury of Eternity not produce in ample abundance the timeless currency of Limitless Light?

Q 257

Primal Explosion

Is not the very first, primal explosion of Light still sounding through the Void, the first existential orgasm of Life?

Cosmic Soughing Sounds

Does the Swan of Soul not breathe Light beautifully,
in and out, in cosmic soughing sounds of So-Ham?

Q 259

The Burning Stitch

Does not the Heavenly Father's bright needle of Light weave throughout the tapestry of a man's gift of Life, the burning stitch of Christ's all-consuming Love for the embodied Soul?

Q 260

Love-Flame

Is it not the innate plan and willed purpose of the Light of Christ, to tenderly guide the ascension of each individual Soul toward the great, all-consuming Love-Flame to be found in the Father's Heart?

Q 261

Cup of Consciousness

How much of the Light can man draw down into his cup of Consciousness, and how much can he practically send upon Its Way, to help Lighten the gravity of darkness?

Q 262

Inexorable Contact

Does not the subjectively scientific arcing of the rainbowed bridge of Light within the disciple's consciousness, help to catalyze the inexorable contact to be had between the Ascending-Self of the disciplined daily life, and that of the Descending-Self, which is almost exclusively taken-up with the concerns of the subtle Spiritual life?

Q 263

Cool Crispness

Does not the cool crispness of the Clear Light coming in from the Soul's profound view of life via the Higher Mind, tend to draw forth from the human peanut gallery some rather typical reactions of 'cold', 'not human', 'no sympathy', 'no true understanding here', 'no love', and 'no heart'... from the emotionally ambiguous light of all who are rooted in the conditional, desire-rooted affections, (and afflictions), of the astral body?

Q 264

Earthly Becoming

Does not your Soul's Essence naturally aspire to a total earthly becoming of the Divine Light?

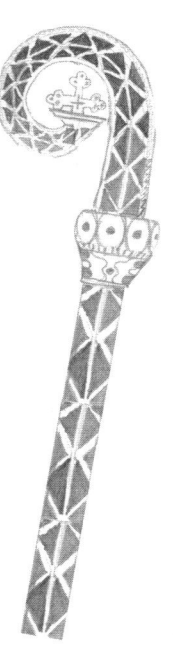

Chapter XXV

Christed-Bâtonship

The Twenty-Fifth Set
of Eleven Contemplative Beads
of Divine Inquiry, bringing into play
the recurrent use of the word
Light

Questions 265 to 275

… Q 265

Particle of Life

In reflecting deeply, can the consciousness of man, beast or thing evolve without Light; and is any particle of life worth living at all, without at least a smidgen of It?

Q 266

Ennui of Life

Does not a constant wrestling with the ennui of life denote but the shortcomings of a fool not being able to see the Light coming in from all sides of where he is?

Q 267

God-Dreamt Purpose

Is it not the Light of the World which weaves the microcosm and macrocosm into an infinitely intricate, definitely interwoven, interdependent Whole of God-Dreamt PURPOSE?

Q 268

'Our Father Who Art In Heaven'

Is not the occult science of 'Divine Monadic Perception' through sapient Soul reflection, the proper and present Aquarian platform upon which the Light of 'Our Father Who Art In Heaven' will eventually stand Revealed, be Envisioned and Loved?

Q 269

'Magic and Ritual'

Is not the Light of Spiritual Evolution soon to toll forth the message of Seventh Ray 'Magic and Ritual' for mankind, and thereby, succeed to establish upon earth the highest of the spiritual sciences for the coming Enlightened Age: that is to say, 'the specific art of the *invocation* and *evocation* of the Divine', for the greater glory and ultimate healing of man?

Q 270

The Great Glittering

Is it possible that in some not too far-distant future, man will attain to the first faint gleamings of the Great Glittering... the Light of which will surpass by far the gilded glistenings of all that constituted the form formerly, even to the sublime grace and subtle shining of the Soul?

Q 271

Collective Consciousness

Will not the Light-inculcated anchoring of the consciousness within the Soul, eventuate in linking the disciple to the united Collective Consciousness of a much Greater Light, called the MONADIC SELF?

Q 272

Solar-wise and Karma-Free

Does not the focussed absorption of the consciousness within the Light of the Soul, eventually put the disciple in touch with his family group of Similar Souls?

Does not this focussed absorption of self into the Light of Soul, also serve the great purpose of duly and dually aligning God's Compassionate Will to the Lighted-Intelligence of the Group SELF, as It impacts upon the world of matter and returns Soular-wise and Karma-free, to Its Alpha-Source in the Subtle Sky, (beyond the three worlds)?

Q 273

Flare of Light

Does not a surprise spark from the central Flame of LIFE often flash a flare of Light into the human heart, to fortuitously uplift and enhearten a Herculean moment of duress, test and trial?

Q 274

Christed-Bâtonship

Is not the supernal Symphonic Orchestration of cosmic 'wheels-within-wheels', and of whole 'worlds-within-worlds' without-end, conducted primarily and paramountly, under the Christed-Bâtonship of the DIVINE LIGHT?

Q 275

Superb Mission

Is not the magnificent Lighting of your whole world with your LIFE, a superb Mission?

Chapter XXVI

Interdimensional Loving

The TWENTY-SIXTH SET
of Eleven Contemplative Beads
of Divine Inquiry, bringing into play
the recurrent use of the word
LIGHT

Questions 276 to 286

Q 276

The Mind's Light

Is there not a parallel between the actual physical illumination of the planet, (as is evidenced throughout the world's great cities and metropolitan areas), and the evolutionary, intelligent point of the enlightened kindling and unfolding of the Mind's Light within Man?

Q 277

Critical Collective Point

Are not the countless Soul-Sparks which make up the Family of Man an innate and intimate part of the evolutionary solar process of Infinite Light expansion; and is not each human being hardily endeavoring to harmonize through the appropriation of conflict (in darkness), to achieve an equitable Peace and a serene Tranquility; and does not man aim to increase his subjective Light to that critical collective point, (so little understood), in Divine Consciousness, called Unconditional LOVE?

Q 278

Joyful Thrust

Are not all the stamped blossoms of specific experiences 'de-Light-fully' undergone able to pass the scrutiny of the Lord of Death in their joyful thrust toward Heavenly Bliss?

Q 279

Deep Pool

Will not the faithful Light at some point in your life, percuss for you a deep pool of Spiritually-inspired prosperity?

Q 280

Windows between Worlds

Is it not GOD's Breathing of the Living Light which actually renders possible the opening of windows between worlds, and which invites the fresh air of one big Common Eternity to Divinely permute the lungs of sentient beings everywhere?

Q 281

Ultra-Conscious Factor

Is not the Light SELF that Ultra-Conscious factor in man, which entices him at rainbow's end to boldly board the Engine of SPIRIT and soar into still higher octaves of Intracosmic Being, and to subjectively implode the ONE HEART into Interdimensional Loving?

Q 282

Scientific Railing

Is it not the responsibility of every man and woman to make the necessary spiritual effort needed to lay down the scientific railing of a Pure Consciousness, which is absolutely required for an ongoing communication with the creative Electrical Energy of the Divine Light... travelling, intradimensionally and alternatively, between the free Soul and the integrated personality of man?

Q 283

Light, Love and Wisdom

Under the dynamic influence of the New Dispensation of 'Cosmic Synthesis and Universal Peace', cannot men and women the world over get together, and bring to Mother Earth a united Human Consciousness... of Light, Love and Wisdom?

Q 284

The Stuff of Light

In the creative manifestation of multifarious profile and posture, of numberless outline and structure, of myriad form and feature, of countless chisel and cut, all made out of the Stuff of Light, is not LIFE Exalted?

Q 285

Sudden Exposure

In the snapshot of any one moment abruptly stopped, is not the Creative Universe without par as a most wondrous sculpture of congealed Light, caught napping in a surprised vibe of Sudden Exposure, or Secret Disclosure?

Q 286

When Peace Reigned Supreme

Are not all men and women of Intuitive Inspiration able to meet somewhere-somehow in the Knowing Light and tap-on through to God's great Unitive Heart; that is to say, are they not able to slip etherically into those grand periods of past ages, to a time when PEACE reigned supreme... and (to) where Peace is even now taking root in the Eternal Present of their SOUL's Infinite Inspiration?

Chapter XXVII

Eternal Time, Synthetic Time

The Twenty-Seventh Set
of Eleven Contemplative Beads
of Divine Inquiry, bringing into play
the recurrent use of the word
Light

Questions 287 to 297

Q 287

Tail of a Cosmic Comet

Is it not the High Lord's LOGOIC Will, (Light-intended by Maitreya the Christ), which is very soon to brightly burst like the Wisdom-tail of a cosmic comet, into all venues of attendant Humanity's exploratory consciousness?

Q 288

The Correct Relationship

On the consummate note of the inner release of the Higher Octaves of Light, will not your Divine SELF reveal to you in perfect clarity the correct relationship existing between Absolute and Relative Time, Synthetic and Artificial Time, Real and Imagined Time?

Q 289

Perfect Mental Mastership

Can it be said that a iberal expression of the emotions does not make a human being necessarily evolve?

The emotions do make him spin around and around in consciousness, desperately so at times, and always in search of that flawless state of Light which will lead him one day, according to his spiritual sadhana, (discipline) and destiny, to a crystal-clear mastery of the emotional body, and finally, to the crowning achievement of perfect Mental Mastership.

Q 290

Every Galaxy's Heart

Is not the Eye of Light also the Silent Inner Witness to the Tranquil Pause, the Breathless State, the Still Centre, the Point of Peace, the Perfect Void, the Utter Emptiness... which is to be found at the burning core of every man's Consciousness, and also, (centripetally), within the double dynamic helix of every Galaxy's Heart?

Q 291

Natural Light Heritage

How come is it, that it takes us so long to learn the so simple lesson of non-identification with sense objects?

And longer still, to put this lesson into practice with the necessary degree of non-attachment required, to take us away from the emotional push-and-pull tyranny, which these sense objects elicit from the body-mind desire machine?

And then, how much longer still, before we finally accede to our natural Light heritage and final Liberation?

Q 292

Half-Way to Heaven

From out of the embers of fiery Love unconditionally given and from the burning Light of selfless Service freely given, does not a man's Spirit reach almost all the way, (at least half-way), to Heaven, in self-Surrendership?

Q 293

Constant Prayer

Since what you lack in understanding is directly proportionate to what you lack in Light, should not your constant prayer be for more and greater Light?

Q 294

'Just As It Is'

Are not mistful, emotional refractions of thought, fanatical idealisms, gross phantasms, twisted misinterpretations, whimsical fancies, vague dreams, astral clairvoyances, romantic fantasies, flighty mystical visions, self-created hallucinations, mediumship trances, and ambitious rainbow-chasings, plus other similar ramblings of "vain human imaginings", all contributory to keeping a man still a thousand Light years away from his truly *seeing* the Bright Absolute 'just as It Is'... unquestionably Grand, positively Pure, Divinely-Clear, and manifestly, (and simply), with no embellishment?

Q 295

Darkness-Dispersing Light

Is there not a critical point attained in the unfoldment of the Spiritual Consciousness where all imagery and vision just simply vanish, or, are abandoned; yet, there solidly exists beyond any possibility of a doubt, the unique realization of the ONE SELF being the sole Radiatory Centre of the darkness-dispersing Light?

Q 296

Scientific Comprehension

Will not the scientific comprehension of the Soul's Light produce one day a literal Lighting-up of the Way out of crude matter by those of Illumined Mind?

Q 297

Sacred Seeds

With applied and humble service to the Christ Light within, are we not in a better position to set up a brotherly rhythm of right relations; and sow everywhere, the sacred seeds of a most sweet goodwill upon the golden fields of human cooperation and creative endeavor?

Chapter XXVIII

God's Surprised Bosom

The Twenty-Eighth Set
of Eleven Contemplative Beads
of Divine Inquiry, bringing into play
the recurrent use of the word
Light

Questions 298 to 308

Q 298

Desire World of Matter

Will the LORD's One Eye of Light triply-blended, eventually and irrevocably destroy the astral vibration in man, thus freeing him from all future bondage to the desire world of matter, mattering?

Q 299

Glamorous Falsity

Is not a key function of the SOUL's 'Eye of Light', the endeavor to properly perceive Essence and lay bare the glamorous falsity of a man's rootless astral light?

Q 300

Angel Lucifer

Under the warrior potency of the Angel Lucifer's lucent and irradiating 'Eye of Light', is not the un-real light of the desire-descended, affection-infected, (overshadowing) thoughtform-aggregate, which is known as the astral plane instantly detected, and its false coloring, deceit and distortion, promptly decried?

Q 301

Noonday Sun

Will not the Soul's eventual and preordained downpour of Light help dissipate all emotional, mental and spiritual suffering in man... in a somewhat similar fashion as to when a multitude of concentrated beams from a diverse number of provisory flashlights enigmatically disappear... as they encounter the intense rays of the noonday sun?

Q 302

The Occult Call

Is it not a natural function of evolution to rhythmically coach and coax the consciousness of a man away from the cloistered confines of his narcissistic personal self; and cycle upon (experiential) cycle, little by little, to cast him spiritually spiraling one fine day upon the Lighted Way, in bowed response to the occult Call of his Higher Evolutionary SELF?

Q 303

God's Surprised Bosom

Is it not the Lighted goal of the unfolding Higher Self along the Evolutionary Path to compassionately extricate man from the labyrinthine shadows of delusion and death; and to thrust him one day, astonished, shocked and gone beyond Mind, unto God's surprised Bosom?

Q 304

Karmic Deadweight

Has not the Holy Spirit avowed to lift from the consciousness of contrite man the karmic deadweight of finite gravity; and pledged to Light-propulse the thoughtfully penitent and now-freed human Spirit into the Divine substantiality of Infinite Grace?

Q 305

Perfect Relatedness

Does the Divine Light not promise to free you indubitably one day from the ubiquitous ignorance of the lower planes; and then, whisk you off de-Light-fully into the Grand Infinitude of a conscious Co-creation, in perfect Relatedness to all things?

Q 306

The Truly Real

Are you not intrinsically prepared for the Light to pluck you out one day from the mirage and play of astral unsubstantiality and to plunk you into the truly Real — finally Revealed?

Q 307

Pin-Point

Is the Soul's Divine Light gently making your trained mind come round to a superb pin-point of crystal-clear concentrated Consciousness?

Q 308

Shamballa's Will

Is not the Great White Brotherhood encouraging Humanity to Light-arc its Consciousness toward the supreme Logoic Design; and conjointly, to cast a serious look with occultly-opened eyes, toward the farsighted Spiritual Plan and Purpose of SHAMBALLA'S WILL?

Glossary

Amrita: A Sanskrit word meaning 'nectar of immortality'.

Anzen: Peaceful Zen; an expression for properly practiced *zazen*, in which body and mind come to a lucidly wakeful calm.

Argus: In Greek mythology, Argus Panoptes, the 'All-seeing'; he was the hundred-eyed giant who was the principle guardian of the divine Nymph Io, Zeus's consort.

Darshan: Being in the presence and receiving the blessing of a holy person.

Dhyana (Dhyanic): Meditation or contemplation; the state of deep stillness and inner poise reached in advanced stages of meditation.

Hong-Sau: A breathing meditation technique (conscious concentration on the breath); the Bengali pronunciation of the Sanskrit mantra, 'Hamsa'; also written as 'So Ham', (I Am That I Am).

Jivatmic (Jivatma): The incarnated Soul; the individualized, human Soul.

Kama-manasic: desire-mind or passion-mind principle.

Karma: Law of cause and effect; action and reaction; 'as you sow, so shall you reap'.

Logos (Logoic): The planetary principle or Creative Deity which manifests through every nation, the peoples, and (five) kingdoms of earth.

Maitreya (Maitreyic): CHRIST as the future World Teacher. He will inspire humanity to see itself as one family and create a civilization based on sharing, economic and social justice, and global cooperation.

Monad (Monadic): The indivisible primordial Self; Spirit Essence; the Divine Womb or Primordial Matrix.

Omkar: OM, the primordial sound resounding rhythmically through the Universe.

Pisces (Triangle of): A rotation and reorientation of the triangular configuration of Pisces-Capricorn-Aquarius; Pisces, (Pilgrim, Probationer, 1st Initiation); Aquarius, (Server, Disciple, 2nd Initiation); Capricorn, (Disciple, Initiate, 3rd Initiation).

Raja yoga: A superior form of yoga meditation, (Raja means royal); it directs the life force, in order to bring the mind and emotions into balance.

Samsara: the cycle of rebirths that a being goes through within the various modes of existence, until final liberation is attained.

Shabd: The Divine Sound Current which is said to be sevenfold in Its expression upon the various planes of Existence, or Consciousness.

Shunyata: Emptiness, Nothingness; Silence; the ultimate Reality as Void, or Voidness.

Sadhak(a): Spiritual aspirant/student; a disciple.

Shamballa: The etheric spiritual centre of the world focussing the Will of God upon planet Earth.

Spanda: A primordial impulse, or pulsation of Creation.

Tisra Til: The third eye, the spiritual eye, or the single eye.

So Be the Light in Our Life

From the Light of being in God
And the Light of being near God

To the Light of being of God
And the Light of being just God

And from the Light of always travelling
From God going to God within God

Do we stand as the Light,
Surrounded by the Light.

Do we stand as more Light
And more Light, and still, as more Light.

And blessed and protected
Are we by that Light,

As we give of the Light
With all of our might,

As we give of the Light
To all in our sight,

As we give of the Light
With all of God's right,

As we are in the Light
In God all a-Bright,

As we ask for the Light
And the Light and the Light,

And so be the Light in our Life.

Orange Palm and Magnificent Magus Publications Inc.©
235 René Lévesque Boulevard East, Suite 310
Montréal, Québec, H2X 1N8 Canada
Telephone: (514) 255-8700
Facsimile: (514) 255-0478
E-mail: info@palmpublications.com
Web site: http://www.palmpublications.com